FLINTS

Flints

DAVID SUTTON

PETERLOO POETS

First published in 1986
by Peterloo Poets
Treovis Farm Cottage, Upton Cross, Liskeard, Cornwall PL14 5BQ

ISBN 0 905291 78 6

Printed in Great Britain by
Latimer Trend & Company Ltd, Plymouth

ACKNOWLEDGEMENTS are due to the editors of *Encounter*, *Poetry Matters*, *A Royal Audience* and *Southern Arts Review* in whose pages some of these poems first appeared.

Cover illustration: Samuel Palmer, 'The White Cloud'. By courtesy of The Ashmolean Museum, Oxford.

For Andrew, Matthew and Jonathan

Contents

Flints

We walk on whiteness, inches under grass.
Few would call it rock: these infant hills,
Brittle as the bones of cuttlefish,
Will never last, they'll flow away like milk
In the next great rain and stain the tide,
And something will be left.
                        We dug a soak-pit,
Chambering the chalk, a well of white
Four foot deep and every bite the spade
Took of that smooth cake the tooth would jar
On something we must pry out: one more stuck
Flour-covered fruit-stone. There they lie, loose-piled,
Just as they'll lie a million years from now
Rubbling some scoured valley. Now my hands
That fought them loose fit lovingly around,
I feel for heft and socket-hollow, thumb
A sleek black shining.
                    Look, a tribe of dour
Dark-skinned aboriginals. They wait
Through bland white epochs, thick-skulled, underground.

At the Open-air Market

The long-haired huckster fans a stack of plates:
One pouring shuffle, like a waterfall.
Smells of crushed grass, frying onions, crates.
A crowd like driftwood builds against his stall.

Housewives, mostly, ready for a lark.
He gets .them going with a tale or two
Then settles to it, looking for a mark.
Beneath the smile his eyes appraise: And you?

Relax, friend. I'm not here to cramp your style.
Purveyors, like consumers, have their rights.
On with the foxy patter; I may smile
But only at a memory that lights

My mind up suddenly, like sun through mist,
Of how you once stole linen from a hedge
In palmy days when young wives could be kissed
Before life set your pugging tooth on edge,

And at another time how plausibly
With what aplomb you preached as you bestowed
Pigs' bones and pardons round the company
In April on the Canterbury road.

Harvest

The field that started where my garden ended
Grew wheat and spring was green, a ribboned rustle
That silvered to the wind. But it was summer
We waited for: to rise in some blue dawn
And find the harvest started; on the hill
The cutter's wake of windrows, blond and glinting
Till baled and stacked they stood again in gold.

Shy as mice, we children watched from hedges
Until the workers went, then out we came
To battle on the slope with stubble-bombs
Or lug the bales to build, like chambered barrows,
Roofed passages where in the ripe hot dark
We sat exchanging stories, intimate,
Remoter from the world than Timbuctoo.

Did seasons last so long in that brown land?
We thought those harvest days would never end
And when they did there was another morning.
Yet autumn came: the wild green clematis
Turned to snow and coal-dust on the hedges,
The jigsaw pattern of the sunbaked paths
Melted, and the paths led out of summer.

Once though, my father took me where the men
Were working in the great barn, stacking up.
I watched them in the sunshot, moted darkness
And thought it then so fine a thing; there was
No play I would not trade to be as these
With salt-stung hands, sharing the harvest honour,
Least of, but known among, that company.

The Computer Room, Midnight

The air's cave-chill. You need two coats in here.
No seasons, nothing varies. Day and night
Walls hum, the white-tiled ceiling casts its light
On racked arrays; all's shadowless and clear.
For here's a place of clarity. And I
Inhabit it; secure I move between
These ordered oracles: see at this screen
I pause with midnight-hollowed eyes to scry:
At once the legend answering appears
Lettered in green fire: initiate,
I understand these matters; I dictate,
The strange beasts purr, obey me. Fifteen years
Of mastering these beautiful unmeanings,
Neat as a titmouse building nests of logic,
Conditioned by reward to run rat-slick
Down these electric mazed meanderings.
Time to go home. I sign the exit page,
Wish the guard good-night. Outside the dark
Is wild: great clouds rise up, a ragged murk
Obliterates the moon's faint silver rage.
I walk the empty roadways, I surrender
To masterless complexities of wind.
Back inside, the snowflakes of my mind
Are melting on the black boots of the future.

Lessons

Watching these minds, more eloquent than mine,
Moved by their varied, passionate intent,
I offer what I can: extend, define,
And give, where nothing else, encouragement,
Silencing the sullen mid-life envy,
My own remembered lack, that says 'Too easy'.

The things I longed for and thought beautiful
Surround them now, and should it not be so?
What parent would not feed his children full
Or having yes within his gift says no?
Who'd teach them to be hungry and alone,
An old dog gnawing at truth's marrow-bone?

The Hillside

A hillside, through the hedge, like holy ground
Gold in evening sun. We find a gap.
The grass is lit or shadowed like a map
With molehill mountains. So, what's this we've found?
Such turf, bush-dotted; flowers everywhere
Like something from the great lament by Clare—

Chalk downland, undisturbed. Too steep for plough?
Yellow with rock-rose, flecked with milkwort's blue,
A knuckled whiteness where the flint shows through,
Here's dyer's greenweed, candytuft, and now
Too much—what's this that opens veiny leaves?
I kneel to it as one who half-believes

His luck at last, then notice by my knee
The level rays of sunset flash on brass:
An empty cartridge, glinting in the grass,
And feathers further on, and now I see
What keeps this place apart: some squire and friends
Down for the pheasant-blasting at weekends.

What's that, you call. Just people, at their games.
No, love, it is not paradise we've found,
But then, where's that on earth's old killing-ground?
My children course the slope, recording names.
I kick the cartridge, whistle them to see
Here where a green-winged orchid holds its plea.

Small Incident in Library

The little girl is lost among the books.
Two years old maybe, in bobble cap,
White lacy tights, red coat. She stands and looks.
"Can't see you, Mummy." Mummy, next row up,
Intent on reading answers absently:
"I'm here, love." Child calls out again: "Can't see."

A large man, his intentions of the best,
Stoops: "Where's Mummy, then?" Child backs away.
Now the tall shelves threaten like a forest.
She toddles fast between them, starts to cry,
Takes the next aisle down and as her mother
Rounds one end disappears behind the other.

I catch the woman's tired-eyed prettiness.
We smile, shake heads. The child comes back in sight,
Hurtles to her laughing, hugs her knees:
"Found you!", in such ringing pure delight
It fills the room, there's no one left who's reading.
The mother looks down, blinking. "Great soft thing."

Blackbird at Dusk, February

Before the lambs and blossom
In the year's first lightening
  A dusk may come,

Not spring yet (frost on grass
Unmelted from the morning)
  But with promise

And something more: one note
Of hope beyond fulfilment
  Where a flute

Plays what all spring's sweet
Green accompaniment
  Cannot repeat.

Frogs

Blob on the lawn.
Black elastic flicker.
Blob on the path and the frogs are back, moving to spawn
In the spring night, travelling
By roads they remember.

Crouched in the dark,
Watching each quick soft rise,
I see in a garden long gone a child stooped to mark
Something unknown, not moving:
A yellow stone with eyes.

Strangeness, delight.
The lost world summons, near,
Softly electric, returning in leaps from the night,
My root-kin, my renewing,
At the spring of the year.

May Day

Walking on the upland, caught by storm,
My son and I this May Day start to race,
Arriving at the same time, wet and warm,
Where valley beeches make a sheltered place.

Gossiping, our backs against a tree,
We listen to the downpour, watch the lane
Lilied with the swirl, dog's mercury
Drip and glister greenly, till the rain

On a sudden stops: grey-silver sky
Smokes northward, driven out by blue; we take
Our way again and move unhurriedly
Uphill just as the sunlight comes to make

A ribbed translucence high above and brings
Earth's odours steaming round us as we go.
Somewhere in the hedge a blackcap sings.
The wet bronze of the maple starts to glow.

Yobs

Me in the rain, my scooter broken down,
Fed up, pushing it, and these four lads
Block the pathway, jeering. Now, why's that?
No idea: for sure they don't know me.
I know them though (villages have eyes):
Petty vandals, go round daubing walls,
Snap the aerials off cars at night,
Wreck the children's playground, damage trees,
Tear the flowers up. Oh, I know them:
Know who's been expelled, in court. I know
Other things: I know who's unemployed,
Who come from broken homes, whose mother went,
Dumped him, four years old, to live with Gran.
I know who loiter now, unreachable,
By wasteland in the rainy winter dusk,
Who cry out "Look at us!"
                                        Not my affair.
I stand then, blocked, aggression's logan-stone
Poised, exquisite.
                                So, who's leader? You,
Tall, in leather jacket, skull-adorned.
"Afternoon. You any good with these?
My baffle-pipe's gunged up, I've sheared the screw."
Silence. Jacket boy considers me.
Thinking what? We've got a right one here?
Puzzled? Wary? I don't know. And then
"Hey, look, what you do ..." "He needs ..." "No, look ..."
Hands in concert, octopoidal, blurring,
Strip, clean out, refit. I clear my throat,
Fumble in my pocket, find two pounds.
"Look, I'd like ..." The leader, kneeling still,
Wipes his oily fingers, straightening,
Hesitates, then smiles and shakes his head.
The scooter starts first time. I ride away.

The Visit

Ahead, the others talked
　　When the bus had set us down.
Four foot tall I walked
　　The unfamiliar town,

And voices in my head
　　Were speaking, grave and clever:
If the known should die, they said,
　　The world will change forever.

That day of blaze and shade
　　The tarry crooked street
Where once my father played
　　Stood empty in the heat.

The terraced house was narrow,
　　The stairs were dark and steep
Where children long ago
　　Went candlelit to sleep.

Stifled in their cases
　　The books inhaled again.
The photographs' dry faces
　　Drank up my youth like rain,

And round and round the table
　　Above the covert ears
The voices like a fable
　　Were sighing for the years.

They might have saved their sighing.
　　For all their child's endeavour
The known has died, is dying.
　　The world is changed forever.

On a Book of Nature Photography

This craft of light, as innocent as Eden!
The earth-star opening, the waterfall
Smoking from the basalt, blue-lit snow,
The wind-borne dust of catkins, green and gold,
A sun-caught fuzz of poppies—how they build,
These pages, to a celebrated world.
Here things speak for themselves within the frame
Of love's attentive silence. What's your text?
No theory you preach but practice, practice.
Beside the images laconic notes
Record a focussed being: angle, stance,
Precisions of the lens, the time of light.

Three for Runners

1.

A lace has come undone.
You kneel by the path in snow,
Aware of windless silence,
The body's pulse and glow.
Black cows by the fence
Stand and steam in sun
That brightens like a halo.
What words has joy? You run.

2.

Alone on the beach at sunset,
The blaze of sun on your face,
You come through the curtains of light
To the lovely remembered place
And move like the mirrored gull,
Weightless, on shining flats.
The atoms of your body
Dance like summer gnats.

3.

Moonlight, rain, the road
A silk of shining gray.
Now all you ever were
And all that you will be
Fall equally away.
You are the road, dim-shadowed,
The leaves of that wet tree,
Glinting and astir.

Postcard from Pembrokeshire

My friends, who go so lightly here and there,
Who jet-propelled, car-catapulted view
Lands, cities, histories and never care
That none of it is yours or speaks to you,
I know you'd laugh to see me here perplexed
Still after two weeks by the rocks and seas
Of one domestic unfamiliar text,
Missing my rooted etymologies
Of Chiltern beech. Yet there's no other way
For us, the slow ones, who would understand
The language of the summer clouds that lay
Their shivering allusions on the land.
We grow like lichen outwards, take an hour
To gloss the gannet's sky-and-ocean glide
Or lost in lexicons of tree and flower
Will walk daylong, while by the waterside
The dancing runes of river-light on slate
All but reveal the lost . . . And summer ends
Before one sentence of it's learnt. Too late,
And yet today, out round the green bird islands
Where seagulls dipped to meet their soaring shadows
On sunlit cliff, it seemed to me I heard
Some phrase, one morning fragment . . . Well, who knows?
I send my love, I'll keep that summer word.

The House Martins

The night we quarrelled I went down to the beach
And twenty martins were there, weaving their flight
Under the sandstone cliffs in the last of the light.
Each had its own niche-moulded nest and each
Would leave in turn to twinkle, skim and dive
Then come like bees re-entering a hive
To hang in folded stillness. It became
Like a compulsion, counting each one back
To fit them in mosaic, white and black
Against the glowing cliff, or like that game
One plays with balls, for as the last flew in
So all the rest would tumble out and spin
In wider circles on the twilit sea.
Nothing I could do would stop that flight
Or lodge the last one in its nest till night
Called the birds back and brought them silently
To rest once more beneath the old scarred rock
That wind and wave had made a butcher's block.

Meetings

Sometimes behind the words of those you meet
You come upon a lost unshareable
Hinterland: some slate-roofed town, mediaeval
In morning light, a suburb in the heat
Of summer dusk, a dalehead where they walked
Between moss-felted walls ... it's there so plain
You step like deer into this new terrain
Until you feel them falter, having talked
Some moments to you gone, so you return
From that deep journey back to surfaces
Yet ever after taste their lives like loss.
How can you tell them this? Unless, in turn,
You meet sometimes another watching too
Behind the words unshareable lost you.

Say

Say that you're at work, and that it's summer.
July. The swifts cry out above the street.
Blinds are drawn against the light-dazed city.
   The office dreams in heat.

Say that there's a quiet dark-haired woman,
(Days like this, a man might fall in love),
With her wide quick smile to walk with you and sit
   At lunch with leaves above.

Say you talk together, oh, of nothing—
Dogs, yoghourt, husbands, children, wives,
Just the way we do that confidential
   Casual trade of lives.

Say you know, for all a million reasons,
Nothing is between you, nor could be,
That she is young, not even to remember
   The hour, your company.

Say you know it, but this day of summer
Touches you as soft as sprinkled rain.
Light, leaves, her green and hazel eyes
   Work in you deep like pain.

Say, returning home, you sit that evening
At twilight under blossom on the grass,
Talking with your wife about your children
   The way such evenings pass.

Say that clarity returns with laughter
For foolish love, but under it despair.
Say you know it now, that pain of sunlight:
   Your youth gone, hard to bear.

Squirrel

Squirrel, like a blob of mercury,
Spills intact through cataracts of tree.

Squirrel's all but bird to nest and fly,
Walks on thin black twigs like cracks in sky.

Squirrel is half tail, a wave of smoke,
A plume, a catkin; squirrel's lord of oak

And walks the copse, not caring if he's seen.
Be prudent, squirrel, keep the trunk between,

But if you must forget, then be as now:
A woodland gargoyle, watching from the bough

As if to ask, "What does it want of me,
That strange, untrustable, two-legged tree?"

A Local History

Digging in his garden, someone found
A Celtic head, green-skinned, with faint smooth hair,
The nose fine-chiselled still, and beautiful
   The falcon stare.

North's the Roman road, but long before
The Ridgeway crossed these hills, oldest of lanes.
Blue cloaks, mud-spattered, gold-torqued warriors.
   The mud remains.

At Englefield the warboats of the Vikings
Startled the herons from their reedy bed.
Alfred attacked, drew back; the cold green river
   Received the dead.

Stephen and Matilda: Wallingford.
The winter land cried out for God's relief.
In the beechwood's grey cathedral trees
   Put forth new leaf.

King Charles's men, through secret furzy ways,
Came south by here to fighting in the town.
Richard Atkyns mourned his men "like fruit
   The wind blows down".

Records for last century: one winter
Five babies dead, winds cold, much frost again.
Water from the ponds, mud floors, the road
   Milky with rain.

Beside the recreation ground a cross:
There died so many, from so small a place.
Still among the old a few remember
   A name, a face.

Nineteen eighty. New estates, new people,
The easeful lives of rootless liberty,
While the stone head watches, and the woods
    Wait silently.

Birds at Pagham

Sunlight on our backs,
　Redshank, dunlin, plover
Braid with looping tracks
　Mud the tide will cover
Brimming to embrine
This level liquid shine.

Out above its flow
　Two herons in their flight
Billow as they slow
　Long-legged to alight.
An avocet, sedate,
Crazed-china-delicate,

Trawls the pond. All's birds:
　The south wind from the sea
Speaks with curlew words
　Of limitless and free
Bright unpeopled plains
Where solitude remains.

Shivered waters glint
　And now from reeds close by
Five arrowheads of flint
　Go spanged across the sky:
Snipe turning in the height
To vanish into light.

Gaia's Dream

Even now, there are places that remember.
Here, where the rocks are rounded to the north
And sleek as seals from that old polishing,
Where valleys end mid-air, sawn-off, and lakes,
Sudden in the hollows under crags,
Flash like kingfishers, the earth will dream.
They come back then. A million blue-white snails
Rasping their way with boulder-studded tongues . . .
Their licks and furrowings disturb her: see,
She shivers in her sleep, the sun has gone,
The wind is from the peak, the lake's still eye
All pupil now stares inward, black, opaque.
Ten thousand years are buried in that blink
And where are we? Diminished, back to scale,
A scattered few, precarious in caves,
Enduring at the edges of her dream.
Again she cradles us with cruel love:
Her latest kind, whom she might come to favour
Or else, tomorrow, might scour off for good.

Valediction

My children grown too old for lap to nestle,
Affection now must play the manly part,
Concealing in the clasp of hands or wrestle
The touch that has been rain to this dry heart,

And I, like all progenitors, discover
Time's paradox: how permanent each stage
Of childhood seems to parents, until over;
Looked back upon, how fleeting all that age.

Now words must take the place of love's first language
Of touch direct and simple as the sun,
And I in colder orbits find the courage
That love must look for, when its work is done.

The Haunted Road

That was the route I loved best
In all my running: a road
Hollow between high banks
Where the farm carts took their load.
The moons of after-harvest
Shone on the dust and showed
Embossed each glinting grain.
The haystack's reek in winter
Was summer's breath again.

That road was haunted, they said:
A tall dark man would glide
Out of the shadows and move
Keeping pace at your side.
A hood would be over his head,
If you spoke he never replied
Till looking down you would see
Whatever walked beside you
Ended at the knee.

No ghosts kept this boy back,
Not then, though the hairs of the young
Rose in the pitch-dark hollows
That the hedges overhung.
So now, shall I fear the track
Or those I walk among,
Though keeping pace they glide:
My escort of the shadows,
The dark man at my side?

Not Daffodils

Less pleasant now, to lie,
Half-dreaming, half-awake,
And watch with inward eye
The images that break.

Not daffodils, my love,
But falcons of remorse
Attend me from above
And track my desert course,

Or water rises fast,
A dark and closing sea,
Where present joins to past
In salt complexity,

Or else that fire, once out,
New-kindled in my brain,
A winter wind of doubt
Extinguishes again.

Air, water, fire: which leaves
Another element.
That image also grieves
And is not heaven-sent.

My love, I hear you claim
It's what you've always said:
That small good ever came
From idling on a bed.

Come then, and exorcise
My vacant, pensive mood
With your clear outward eyes.
People my solitude.

Another Small Incident

November evening, rain outside and dark
Beyond the building's honeycomb of warmth.
The old man stands there, waiting to be noticed.
He wears propitiation like a coat.
The girl looks up at him. "Yes? Can I help you?"
"This card you sent like, that's the problem, see.
It says I've got your book, but that's not right.
I mean, I had it but I brought it back.
That's what I do, I read one, bring it back.
I never keep them, see."
                                    He stands, condemned
Yet quivering for justice. "All right, sir."
She smiles at him. "We get mistakes like that.
Just leave the card with me." He stares at her,
Seventy, with spotted hands, afraid,
And someone smiles at him and calls him sir.
Lighting at the contact, like a bulb,
He warms to her. "That's what I do, you see.
I take the one, I read it, bring it back.
I thought, you know, it might be on the shelves.
I mean, if no one's had it since like, see."
Another girl comes by. "We're closing, Sue.
You coming?" Sue looks up and rolls her eyes.
The old man catches it. He understands.
He turns and shuffles out into the night.

Marathon Man

On stone-hard spirits, lichen.
How do they fare when it starts,
When the legs fail and the heart's
Great labour flags? What then?

But you, John, stayed the same
For dying you ran still
Though slowed by death's long hill,
On which last road you came

To a place known to few
Beyond all hope and pride
And did on that far side
Such things as you could do.

Outskirts

Someone should speak of these peculiar margins,
Neither town nor country, where nobody goes.
The cornfields seem abandoned, yet corn grows.
The pasture's shaggy, like a firing-range.
Who cares for this, who keeps it? One begins
To wonder sometimes. I have stood at twilight
Watching swifts around an empty grange,
Black boomerangs, returning in their flight,
So close their wings have clipped me. There's a fear
About this. Where has everybody gone?
Almost comforting the ridged horizon
Contains the motorway's lit pouring sea.
Even so, I do not go too near.
It would not do to risk a certain sight,
No traffic there but wind, and endlessly
The shining pistils stretching into night.

Stellar Sequence

Young stars begin to burn as though
   There were no limit to their light
And they alone were charged to show
   An old defiance to the night.

In middle years the helium
   Contracts but now in novel ways
From dark disequilibrium
   Some breed a self-consuming blaze.

These shells of radiance depart.
   They sink upon themselves again.
A pulse reveals the signal heart
   That chafes in its compacted pain,

As now with all their lustre spent
   They turn to night a secret face
Yet grow in their diminishment
   Till time is bent about their place.

Dune Country

Crouched, I become the land
Flexing its lion shoulders. The light torments me.
Something's far out, it dazzles on the sea.
  The wind comes, driving sand
Minute by minute, bearing my substance away.
How shall I root and stay?

  I stand my shifting ground.
I build defences, knit with marram, heal with moss.
The sift, the scurry, whisperings of loss
  Continue all around.
These brambles with their blood-dark leaves, their fruits are mine.
They taste of mud and brine.

  Gulls glitter in the height.
Men, when they come, are the odd ones, walking alone.
The sea brings driftwood, delicate as bone.
  I drum to gales of light.
Wind tears my roots, throws down my building, all's in vain.
I lie low, try again.

Something Else

Once a day, at lunch time, for an hour
I leave the small hot cabin where I work
To walk this land between the road and river
Unclaimed, or little used: where fields of grass
That nothing grazes flank a muddy footpath
Beside which runs a culvert filled with brambles,
Tyres and stagnant water.
                                        I have found
Nothing here remarkable, unless
One counts last winter's snowdrifts on the bank,
Lipped and fluted, like great smooth-gilled fungi,
Or else the flocks of gulls that came to feed
Beside the shining thaw, and always rooks'
Black flaking storms, or pigeons' floating silver
Between the poplars.
                                    Nothing then, and yet
Something has happened: like a child returning
Affection never known the land has answered
My love's wry constancy: the blackbird now
Sips at the puddle while I pass, the bank vole
Patters from the ditch, and I have found
In spring marsh marigolds beneath the bridge,
Gold on dark green, in that place a thing
Amazing: giver and receiver both,
The land and I, stand back in gratitude.
We know survival; this is something else.

October Fungi

They are back again, the people of the woods,
A travelling circus of freaks: they have pitched their camp
On meadows of moss between the boles of beeches.
There's no concealment here: they loll on stumps
In sulphur tribes or swagger in the leaves
Scarlet as outlaws. Fear is in their names:
Destroying Angel, Deathcap, Sickener.
The darkness bred them, devilry's their lore
And parody their style. There's Dryad's Saddle
Perched, a monstrous butterfly of leather;
This velvet sleek translucence is Jew's Ear,
There's blewit's ghostly lilac, polypores
Rubber-tough or textured like meringue,
Smelling of peach and honey. So we meet
Towards another year's end in the woods.
What shall I say to you, gay-sinister
Consorts of corruption? Welcome, life.
The slugs have gorged themselves on stinkhorn jelly
And here's a puffball ready to explode,
A wrinkled cerebellum, parchment-yellow,
A rotted sack of flour that splits and spills.
The spores rise up, dream-delicate, like smoke.
They glint and dwindle down the shining air.

Anniversary

A rapids-rider, finding this brief stay,
No more perhaps than where the waters gather
In amber calm before the next cascade,
I turn and see, surprised at my surprise,
(Unthinkable it could be otherwise)
That you're here too: have threaded your own way,
So close yet separate, by shoot and boulder
Through the daze and din of time's white water.

You smile again with that old innocence.
I think: the springs of youth did not foretell
These cataracts ... I dreamed you swan-like, made
To drift beneath green courtesies of willow,
Your cygnet brood unendingly in tow.
What brought you then to such a turbulence,
Time or I? Yet we are here; the swell
Draws our craft together. All is well.

Lost

A joke among the family: how father
Gets them lost, then cheerful in disgrace
Speaks for the virtue of the unplanned venture,
The vagrant interlude, the unsought place.

Who found the fallow deer, the brambly clearing
Where berries hung their tartan tapestry?
Who came out on the cliffs that April morning
Above the hammered silver of the sea?

Ah, but had they come where they were going,
Then what would they have seen, their counter goes,
While he pursues the path of his unknowing,
To "Where's this?" answering "God only knows".

Finders Keepers

All was to be revealed,
  Labelled and exact,
As on some site lies peeled
  Each layered artefact,

But memory, you prove
  No archaeologist
So patiently to move
  No crumb of life is missed.

The flashing random spade
  Ungovernably delves.
Who thought to see displayed
  Such debris of lost selves?

Stranger, should there glint
  Upon this ruined scene
Among the clay and flint
  Amazingly washed clean

Some relic, then receive,
  If lost indeed be found,
The right of trove I leave
  To this my troubled ground.

Audit

Being middle-aged is closing doors.
You owe too much: consider the expense.
The sign the people look for is not yours.
These rooms that you keep ready—where's the sense
With guests so seldom? Come, abate your pride,
Confess it now: this is not justified.

Then pull the covers over, draw the blind,
Look round for one last time, and turn the key.
They never came, the ones who might have dined,
So was it loss, that hospitality?
Disdain such reckoning, though doubt and age
Are frowning at the items on the page.